MW00634746

THE

BAT

HOUSE

GUIDE

THE BAT HOUSE GUIDE

BY MERLIN TUTTLE AND DANIELLE CORDANI

MERLIN TUTTLE'S BAT CONSERVATION

GREENLEAF
BOOK GROUP PRESS

Page 2 Millions of Brazilian free-tailed bats emerging from Frio Cave in Texas can be seen for miles.

Page 4 Pallid bats help ranchers by consuming large numbers of grasshoppers and crickets.

Page 6 Single colonies of Brazilian free-tailed bats consume tons of insects nightly and save Texas farmers millions of dollars annually.

Page 8 Inspecting paired bat houses in Florida, protected from midday heat by an overhanging roof.

Page 11 A Northern long-eared bat emerges from roost beneath loose bark in Tennessee.

Page 12 Long-tongued bats pollinate many important tropical flowers and are easily attracted to live in tower roosts made of mixed concrete and sawdust.

Published by Greenleaf Book Group Press
Austin, Texas
www.gbgpress.com

Distributed by Greenleaf Book Group

For ordering information or special discounts for bulk purchases, please contact Greenleaf Book Group at PO Box 91869, Austin, TX 78709, 512.891.6100.

Design and composition by Pentagram, Austin
All images copyright Merlin Tuttle unless otherwise stated.

Publisher's Cataloging-in-Publication data is available.

Print ISBN: 978-1-62634-981-0

eBook ISBN: 978-1-62634-982-7

Part of the Tree Neutral® program, which offsets the number of trees consumed in the production and printing of this book by taking proactive steps, such as planting trees in direct proportion to the number of trees used: www.treeneutral.com

Printed in Canada on acid-free paper

22 23 24 25 26 27   10 9 8 7 6 5 4 3 2 1

First Edition

TABLE OF CONTENTS

Merlin Tuttle photographing emerging free-tailed bats in Texas (Photo courtesy of Teresa May Nichta).

Dear Friend of Bats,

It has been nearly 40 years since I introduced Americans to bat houses. Thanks to the creativity of numerous private citizens and professional colleagues, and the generosity of our members, much progress has been made. This publication represents the combined wisdom of America's most experienced bat house pioneers, involving thousands of houses from coast to coast. Here, Danielle Cordani and I review their findings as of 2020.

We found broad agreement on key determinants of success, though preferences for specific materials and treatments sometimes differed markedly. Clearly, we still have much to learn. In this resource we share areas of agreement, attempt to explain differences of opinion, and suggest areas for further experimentation.

Artificial roosts should not be used to justify further loss of natural ones. However, where natural roosts cannot be replaced, alternatives can be extremely important. Bat houses should be built to last for as long as possible. Nevertheless, even ones available for just a few years can help bats who often have few, if any, remaining options.

Perhaps most importantly, bat houses provide powerful tools for neighborhood education, demonstrating the values of living in harmony with nature. Attracting bats can be lots of fun and can contribute to a healthier environment.

Please help bats protect our future. By joining Merlin Tuttle's Bat Conservation, you will support ongoing bat house research, keep up with the latest discoveries of bat values and needs, and receive invitations to join us in events and workshops worldwide.

Sincerely,

Merlin Tuttle
Founder & Executive Director
Merlin Tuttle's Bat Conservation

SCAN FOR MORE INFO OR VISIT

https://www.merlintuttle.org/i-want-to-help/

WHY DO WE NEED BATS?

Worldwide, bats are masters at keeping populations of night flying insects in balance. In tropical and subtropical areas, they additionally rank among nature's most effective pollinators and seed dispersers. Their loss could threaten whole ecosystems and our survival. Nevertheless, current numbers are often small fractions of those needed to protect a healthy planet.

Mosquito Reduction

Nothing can eliminate mosquitoes, but bats can help. Just one little brown myotis can consume 1,000 or more mosquito-sized insects in a single hour, and bats can significantly reduce numbers of egg-laying females. Recent research at the University of Wisconsin found that big brown bats and little brown myotis, living in bat houses, were consuming far more mosquitoes than previously realized, including 15 species, 9 of which carry West Nile virus.

Crop Protection

In southern and western North America, Brazilian free-tailed bats are among the most frequent bat house users. They consume vast quantities of migratory moth pests. A colony of big brown bats from just one bat house can consume enough cucumber beetles to prevent millions of eggs from being laid on gardens or crops in a single summer. Nationally, bats save U.S. farmers nearly $23 billion annually. Worldwide, insectivorous bats protect a wide variety of crops, including rice, corn, cotton, cocoa, coffee, and macadamia nuts. Researchers in the Mediterranean documented that strategic placement of bat houses around rice paddies could gradually eliminate the need for pesticides. South African macadamia growers are testing bat houses to protect orchards against green stink bugs.

Pollination and Seed Dispersal

Throughout tropical and subtropical areas, bats that pollinate flowers and disperse seeds are essential to the health of entire ecosystems and service crops that are valued at billions of dollars annually. Even these bats can benefit from artificial roosts in Latin America.

Small bats such as this short-nosed fruit bat in Southeast Asia are key pollinators for wild banana plants.

HOW CAN YOU HELP BATS?

Millions of free-tailed bats emerging from Bracken Cave, Texas, provide one of nature's most spectacular events.

Bats are essential, but populations are in alarming decline nearly everywhere, often due to loss of natural roosts. Countless colonies have lost their homes as forests have been cleared, caves have been converted for human use, and fearful humans have killed or evicted those attempting to take refuge in buildings. However, by simply providing accommodations, you may help dozens, hundreds, or even thousands of destitute bats. As many Americans are discovering, bats provide safe pest control, unique entertainment, and outstanding educational opportunities. Attracting bats may be easier than you think!

Thousands of little brown myotis and big brown bats are relying on bat houses as they slowly recover from more than a decade of massive losses from white-

nose syndrome. Private citizens are helping some of the hardest hit species recover. Dramatic recovery has often been achieved through provision of artificial roosts or restoration and protection of damaged roosts. Rapid growth of colonies in bat houses strongly suggests that roost shortage is a key impediment to their recovery.

The Florida bonneted bat, believed to be extinct for more than a decade, was rediscovered in 1978 living in a backyard bat house. This species is now recovering in small, easy-to-build bat houses.

The more you learn about bats, the more you can help. Share your personal experience with friends and neighbors. Helping people overcome needless fear of bats is key to their survival.

A nursery colony of fringed myotis reared young beneath loose bark on this old snag in Arizona.

GETTING STARTED

The nearer you live to a river, lake, or wetland, especially where natural vegetation remains, the greater the odds of attracting bats. Such areas are prime breeding grounds for reliable and diverse insect prey that can sustain colonies at times when yard or crop pests are not available. Bat houses are least likely to attract occupants in areas of intense urbanization or industrialized agriculture.

Single-chamber houses being built to test bat needs.

Depending on the bat species where you live, there may be a variety of options for bat house success. Bats attempting to live in buildings or other man-made structures is a good indicator of suitable feeding habitat nearby. Well-built and located bat houses are more than 80% successful, rising to 90% where colonies have been excluded from buildings.

Choosing a First-time Bat House

Prior to building or purchasing bat houses, one should always evaluate potential locations and methods of mounting. Once you've found appropriate locations, many options are available, ranging from simple to complex.

Rivers and their associated natural vegetation provide ideal feeding opportunities for bats.

This three-chamber bat house became overcrowded with free-tailed bats within just a few days.

Single-chamber bat houses have long been viewed as minimally attractive to bats, in part because vendors have frequently sold ones that were destined to fail due to poor construction and/or inadequate instructions.

When painted different colors, or located in different amounts of sun, two or more single-chamber houses may meet as well as test bat needs better than one multi-chamber house and thus prove more attractive. Providing varied options roughly doubles the odds of success. Multiple houses allow bats to move in response to changes in weather or to escape parasites or predators.

Once local needs are known, attracting larger numbers is often easy and can be lots of fun. Also, keep in mind that there are often additional species in need whom you might help with a bit of extra experimentation. Whether you choose to build or buy, there is no one bat house for all circumstances. It is wise to consider personal goals as well as key criteria for attracting bats prior to investing in any bat house.

SCAN FOR MORE INFO OR VISIT

https://www.merlin-tuttle.org/selecting-a-quality-bat-house/

Ready-Made

Quality bat houses are available, either ready-made or as kits. We certify only those that meet the following minimum criteria:

- Landing and roosting surfaces roughened
- Most roosting chambers 3/4" to 7/8" wide
- All outer connections caulked or glued
- External surfaces sealed or painted
- Vents to reduce risk of overheating
- Detailed and adequate instructions

The best vendors provide such specifications on their websites.

Bat house kits are easy to assemble.

Do-It-Yourself

If you choose to build your own, providing a bat house for bats may require no more tools than a saw, screwdriver, and paint brush. Depending on your level of interest and available mounting locations, you might consider two or three easy-to-build, single-chamber houses.

The detailed bat house instructions we provide are simply intended as starting guides. Most houses can be substantially enlarged or improved once you understand bat needs. We also introduce a wide range of options from around the world and strongly encourage testing of new materials, designs, and ideas.

Nut growers from California to Texas and Georgia increasingly are using bat houses in pest management.

Comparing houses of different sun exposure provides key insight into local bat needs.

Bats seek summer homes that provide a comfortable range of temperature, are leak- and draft-free, safe from predators, and located as near as possible to food and water. Thus far, most American-made houses have accommodated only crevice-roosting species, though additional options have potential. Advances in knowledge often have come from those who broke presumed rules for success, so testing of new ideas is encouraged.

Temperature

Temperature is a key determinant of bat house success. Needs vary according to species, reproductive condition, local weather, and season. This may sound complicated, but at any given location even two or three simple houses may prove enlightening.

> Harry Harnish reported a nursery colony of big brown bats in Arkansas that, for 10 years, consistently used a bat house in a sunny location. However, during a summer of extreme heat, this colony moved to a previously unoccupied house in the shade.

Start by providing two or more single-chamber houses, each exposed to differing amounts of sun or painted and vented to absorb and retain varied amounts of heat.

Positioning houses near one another makes it easier for bats to move back and forth in response to changing conditions. Needs also vary among species. For example, big brown bats and Indiana myotis consistently choose cooler roosts than little brown myotis.

Nursery colonies require extra warm roosts, ideally ranging from 80° to 100° F when bats are present. Heat comes either from the sun or from clustered mothers. Using body heat to raise roost temperature is costly for bats, so roosts that minimize this need are especially attractive. Nevertheless, if houses overheat, flightless young can be killed, especially those of free-tailed bats who are least able to carry pups to new locations.

Strategically placed vents can greatly diminish this risk. Vents are most needed in moderate to hot climates. They are generally located in approximately the lower third of fronts or sides, often higher in backs. The higher the vents, the greater the cooling effect. Where overheating is detected (bats exposing themselves at roosting crevice entries on hot days), overcrowding could be the problem. If so, the most effective remedy may be an additional nearby house. As an added precaution, the new one may be better vented, lighter in color, or less exposed to the sun. Where bats leave for winter, and aren't overcrowded, just painting the original house a lighter color may be sufficient.

Maps of regional temperature are often used to guide selection of an appropriate bat house color or amount of sun. Nevertheless, there are no absolutes. The color needed to meet bat requirements will vary substantially based on both the angle and length of daily sun exposure.

An ideally located nursery house in Florida (Photo courtesy of Bat Conservation and Management).

The hottest locations require the least sun and lightest colors, while the coolest require the most sun and darkest colors. Where high temperatures average 80° to 100° F in July, the appropriate color may vary from light to dark with sun exposures of approximately 3 to 7 hours. Where temperatures seldom reach 80° F, bats will prefer medium to dark houses and 7 to 10 hours of sun. Providing multiple houses of varied color or sun exposure may prove critical to survival during weather extremes.

In Wisconsin, Kent Borcherding often paints houses medium brown, changing to black for the top 8" to 10". In houses built for use in all but the hottest climates, John Chenger uses extra thick, black roofs on lighter brown houses. In Georgia and Florida, Frank Bibin and Thomas and Laura Finn protect against midday heat by providing light-colored metal roofs that have 4" to 10" of overhanging eaves. They also leave a 7/8" space beneath the overlapping metal roof to increase ventilation and roosting space.

Mounting Location

Most bats prefer roost locations within 50 feet of trees and hedgerows, but at least 20 feet from the nearest limbs, or other potential hawk or owl perches. Mixed habitats, especially along forest borders within a quarter mile of streams, rivers, or lakes, are ideal (illustrated below). Windy areas and locations near tall, thorny vegetation should be avoided.

Cal Butchkoski reported that, in Pennsylvania, where little brown myotis had to fly more than 50 feet to reach tree cover, they suffered from increased screech owl and hawk attacks.

The most successful bat houses are mounted on buildings or poles. Houses mounted on trees are often too shaded or vulnerable to predators and are less than half as well used.

In areas where day-to-night temperatures shift by more than 28° F (mostly in arid locations) bat houses are seldom used

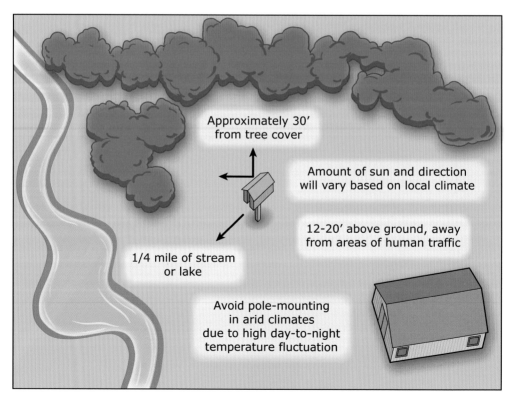

Approximately 30'
from tree cover

Amount of sun and direction
will vary based on local climate

12-20' above ground, away
from areas of human traffic

1/4 mile of stream
or lake

Avoid pole-mounting
in arid climates
due to high day-to-night
temperature fluctuation

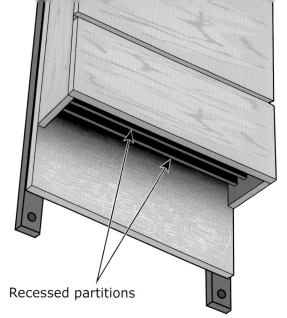

Recessed partitions

Predator Avoidance

Most bats give birth to just one pup per year, making predation exceptionally serious. Risks are often lowest when houses are mounted on buildings, highest when mounted on trees that are easily climbed by raccoons and other predators. Rat snakes are excellent climbers and can pose special problems. Especially where they occur, pole-mounted houses should be protected with a predator guard made from 1/4" hardware cloth shaped like an inverted funnel and positioned about 4 feet above ground (illustrated below). Exclusion devices to protect purple martins also work for bats.

> Laura Finn has a novel approach to snake problems. She simply coats metal poles with a foot-wide band of Vaseline at chest height every two months, or as needed.

unless mounted on buildings, which stabilize temperature. Masonry or stone structures are preferred due to their superior thermal stability. East-facing locations receive morning sun and afternoon shade, appropriate for many hot climates. Houses facing south provide extra heating needed in cooler climates. Locations over windows, doors, or walkways, or where odor could be objectionable, should be avoided.

Pole-mounting enables avoidance of locations where droppings from hundreds of bats could become a nuisance. This method also facilitates placement for best sun exposure, emergence viewing, and predator protection. Extraordinary success has been achieved in moderate to hot climates when houses are mounted in back-to-back pairs on poles, protected by an overhanging metal roof. Mounting houses 3/4" to 7/8" apart, with roughened backs, provides an additional well-ventilated roosting chamber with less risk of overheating. Positioning pairs of houses to face southeast and northwest promotes an optimal range of solar heating.

Ideally, houses should be mounted with bat entries at least 10 feet above the ground or any vegetation. Free-tailed bats are less maneuverable than other species and prefer houses 12 to 20 feet above the ground.

By extending the front and sides of multi-chambered bat houses to be 3" to 4" longer than roosting partitions (illustrated above) bats can be protected when entering and exiting, and when exposing themselves on extra hot days. Also, avoid placing bat houses near owl nesting boxes and within 20 feet of potential hawk or owl perches.

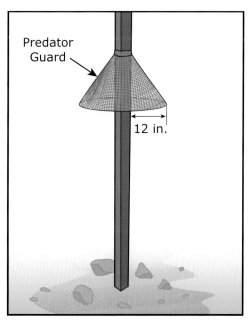

Predator Guard

12 in.

A Swainson's hawk catching Brazilian free-tailed bats.

House Size and Shape

No bat house design is ideally suited for all locations or species. Nevertheless, more than a dozen North American species have been attracted to the houses here recommended.

Cube-shaped houses are less likely to overheat but often do not absorb enough heat to meet bat needs, especially in cool climates. Flatter houses expose more surface area to sunlight, enabling greater heat absorption.

Ideally, most houses should be at least 20" to 24" tall. Tall houses provide the best thermal gradients, ranging 20° F or more from top to bottom, especially when aided by vents. This allows bats to move vertically to adjust to daily and seasonal changes. Wider, shorter houses gain solar heat faster and may attract more bats during cooler spring weather. However, they risk overheating in summer.

Large bat houses provide greater temperature stability and can shelter more bats. However, they also can be stable in the wrong temperature range, often too cool, resulting in failure to attract bats. Initially small numbers of bats may not be able to heat a large house. Many successful bat house builders began by experimenting with smaller houses of varied temperature,

then gradually provided more or larger accommodations as populations grew.

The largest houses often take longest to attract first occupants, even where they ultimately shelter more bats.

Roosting Crevices

Most bats in temperate regions will occupy roosting spaces 3/4" to 7/8" wide. However, the largest crevice-roosting species, for example Florida bonneted, pallid, and big brown bats, often prefer crevices 1" to 1-1/2" wide. Big brown bats commonly share multi-chambered houses with smaller species and use cooler rear chambers 7/8" to 1" wide.

Spacers should be provided between roosting partitions at 12" to 16" intervals to prevent warping as shown below. Successful bat house builders disagree on whether roosting partitions should reach ceilings.

In Florida, Thomas and Laura Finn believe leaving gaps above roost partitions allows young to cluster and share body heat while mothers are away feeding. In contrast, Terry Lobdell in Pennsylvania securely attaches partitions to ceilings to increase the range of temperature between roosting spaces. Both have been successful.

Some of the more than 1,200 little brown myotis attracted to six nursery houses mounted on a New York barn (Photo courtesy of Caroline Van Kirk Bissell).

A "Bat Barn" at the University of Florida, Gainesville. Though ultimately successful, improved designs are needed.

The 18-foot-square "Bat Barn" Merlin designed for the University of Florida, Gainesville, was completed in April 1991. But, despite exclusion of thousands of free-tailed bats from other university structures, it took two years to attract the first 7 bats, four years to attract a nursery colony of 200, and five years to attract 3,000. By the sixth year, the colony suddenly jumped to 60,000, and grew to 200,000 by 2009. When emergence viewing became popular, two more similar structures were added, and the colony was estimated to be approaching 500,000 by 2020.

We can only speculate on the long-delayed, but ultimately dramatic success. The 3/4"-wide roosting crevices were shielded from solar heating by a large attic above and probably were not ideally warm for rearing young. Nevertheless, as numbers grew, shared body heat likely compensated. It is possible that smaller houses with more surface area exposed to sun would have warmed faster and attracted occupants sooner.

Secure Footing

Roughened surfaces are essential for secure footing. Like temperature, roughness is a key element in determining bat house success, especially on roosting partitions and landing areas. Many builders simply roughen surfaces by scratching them in a circular motion, using a hand-sized block of wood with several protruding screws (illustrated below).

Some of the most successful houses we've seen had at least 1/2" thick solid wood for landing pads and roosting partitions with

Though they do not use traditional bat houses, nursery colonies of up to two hundred Rafinesque's big-eared bats have been attracted to tower roosts constructed of cinderblocks.

horizontally cut grooves 1/8" to 1/16" deep at 1/4" to 3/4" intervals. However, when partitions and landing pads are made of plywood, grooves should not be cut more than approximately 1/32" deep to avoid causing early deterioration.

Many large building supply stores carry 7/8" or 1" thick cedar that is "rough-cut" on one or both sides. This can provide outstanding footing and thermal stability but is more difficult to work with and heavier to mount.

Greg Tatarian coats one surface of each of his roosting panels with widely available lapis lustre sand. This type is chosen for its rounded, non-abrasive texture. Other similarly rounded options are often available locally at landscaping and garden supply stores (recommended size is #2-20). He coats each interior panel with marine-grade-2-part epoxy, thinned 15% with acetone to promote penetration into the wood while still retaining enough viscosity to grip the sand. He applies it by tossing handfuls at an angle across the wet, epoxy-coated panels. The goal is a light application—just enough to provide grip without being too abrasive or heavy.

Bats seem to especially like houses with landing pads and roosting partitions that are tightly covered in vinyl-coated polyester pet-proof window screen. However, weak products, often too loosely applied, have led to many problems and warnings against use. Warnings aside, some especially successful bat houses include quality screen properly attached.

Terry Lobdell's first bat house, put up in 1999, with fiberglass window screen attached to one side of each plywood roosting partition, has consistently ranked among his best used nursery houses for 21 years and remains in good condition. The screen was attached by first applying vertical rows of clear silicone caulking, 1-1/2" apart, then firmly pressing the screen into the caulk. He later successfully used Phifer's vinyl-coated fiberglass pet resistant mesh attached with stainless steel staples. He now finds it easier and less expensive to simply use rough-cut lumber.

Only spray paint or diluted stain should be applied to landing and roosting areas to avoid smoothing rough surfaces. Matte black is preferred for internal use as it reduces light reflection and may encourage occupancy.

Self-Cleaning

Bat houses should be self-cleaning. In other words, droppings should not accumulate inside. Open bottoms permit self-cleaning and seem ideally suited to houses with vented cooling in warm to hot climates. In cooler areas, providing bottoms that slope 45° or more can increase temperature stability while still providing some self-cleaning. Such bottoms should be hinged at the top to facilitate annual inspection.

Wasp Management

Roost widths of 3/4" are least attractive to wasps, a good reason for mostly using widths no greater than 7/8". Wasps are mainly a problem in houses not yet occupied by bats. However, accumulated nests should be removed after carefully checking to ensure bats aren't present. Mud daubers are seldom aggressive and have weak stings. Their nests are easily removed with a 1/2" diameter piece of conduit. Paper wasps are aggressive and have painful stings. Their nests are best removed on cold days in mid-winter. If wasps take over a bat house in summer, nests can be removed if temperatures fall below 55° F. Bats will tolerate a few small wasp nests, but if a crevice becomes fully lined the bats will leave.

General Maintenance

Annual checkups are recommended, normally after bats have left for the winter. Remove wasp nests or other blockages and repair any woodpecker damage. Also, remove tree limbs encroaching within 20 feet, or plant life more than two feet tall beneath. Houses last much longer if re-caulked and painted at several-year intervals when bats are not present.

Guano may be periodically removed and used as powerful fertilizer on potted or garden plants. Just be careful not to stir up and inhale dust from either bat or bird droppings, as they could contain spores of the fungus *Histoplasma capsulatum*. This widespread fungus normally causes asymptomatic or mild cold-like symptoms but can be serious if inhaled in large quantities or by an immuno-compromised person.

Periodic tree trimming may be necessary to prevent encroachment (Photo courtesy of Bat BnB).

MOUNTING YOUR BAT HOUSE

Poles

Sixteen-foot pine poles, both pressure-treated and untreated, are widely available from building supply stores. Untreated hardwood poles are strongest, longest lasting, and may be obtained from independent sawmills. Steel poles with inside diameters of 2" or larger are available in 20' to 24' lengths from pipe supply and plumbing companies. House height can be increased by use of pivot-pole mounting systems (illustrated right). Most bat houses can be adapted for mounting on either wooden or metal poles.

Where untreated hardwood poles are unavailable for use in rocket boxes (see Appendix 2, p. 64), we suggest two 8' poles, one treated and the other untreated. They can be spliced together with the untreated one on top to avoid exposing bats to toxins. Four-inch-square wooden poles are sufficient for lighter houses, but 4" x 6" are best when heavier or paired houses are used.

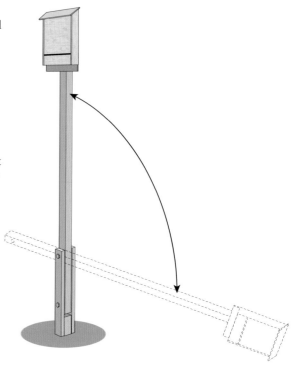

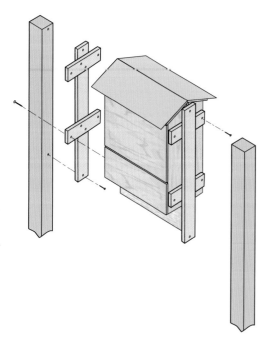

In Florida, Thomas and Laura Finn build a paired combination into a single house mounted atop a 2" x 2" x 24' square, steel pole, which they reinforce by inserting a 12' x 1-5/8" schedule 40 pipe. This dual pipe system is designed to support a 70-pound house to withstand 137 MPH winds. For corrosion resistance, they sand and treat poles with Ospho (a rust inhibitor), then apply two coats of galvanized metal primer such as Kilz and two coats of exterior latex paint.

Pairs of houses can be mounted back-to-back on opposite sides of a single 4" x 6" wooden or 2" steel pole. However, we recommend attaching them to each other 3/4" to 7/8" apart, jointly protected by a metal roof. This provides another roosting chamber, an improved range of temperature, and increases house longevity. Additional roosting space can be provided if spacers are used to raise the metal roof 3/4" to 7/8" above the wooden roofs.

Mounting on crossbeams between poles is a relatively easy and popular means of providing and testing multiple houses in a convenient and secure location.

All poles should be embedded in 3' to 4' deep holes, 14" or more in diameter, depending on soil hardness. Softer soils may require a wider base. Poles should be 5' to 6' longer than the planned installation height. A pair of poles is often used for mounting two houses back-to-back (illustrated bottom left).

Several inches of small rocks or gravel should be added to hole bottoms to facilitate drainage. While poles are held in place, a level should be used to ensure a vertical set, and a compass should be checked for southeast and northwest orientation. Gradually add Quickrete concrete mix, alternately dumping 1/3 of the concrete mix and small amounts of water into the hole, mixing with a digging bar. Once a half-bag of concrete is in the hole, the post will be exceedingly difficult to adjust further. Braces may not be required, as the concrete quickly sets. Mound the concrete slightly at the base of the pole to facilitate drainage.

Houses can be attached to steel poles using carriage bolts, but this necessitates cutting or drilling holes into metal. U-bolts require no special tools. For a single house, attach two 1" x 4" horizontal crosspieces to the back, then one vertical 1" x 6" mounting board. To mount pairs of houses, use two 1" thick crosspieces along each of the two sides to hold them together. Then attach a 1" x 6" vertical mounting (or shade) board screwed over the cross pieces on each end for attachment to poles.

In Wisconsin and Kentucky, Kent Borcherding and Dan Dourson highly recommend black locust or oak posts. Kent reports black locust can remain sturdy for more than 50 years.

A sloping, 4' long trench can facilitate easier raising of bat houses mounted on poles.

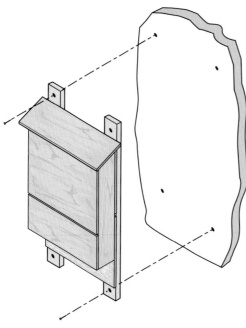

boards long enough to extend 3" to 4" beyond the top and bottom of the house, and securely attach them along each side on the back illustrated left. Then use these for attachment.

Extend a ladder to just below the intended mounting location. The tools and house may be raised separately on cords. The bottom of the house can be braced on the upper end of the ladder to hold it steady during attachment, using outdoor screws appropriate for the substrate. We suggest hiring a professional unless you are fit and experienced.

The French Cleat

The French cleat, shown below, is often preferred for its ease of attachment. To create the cleat, cut two 1" x 4" pieces of lumber that extend the full width of the bat house, each with a 30° beveled edge. Using deck screws, attach one piece to the back of the bat house, and the other to the wall from which the house will be hung, forming a matching cleat. Next, use deck screws to attach another 1" x 4" piece of lumber along the back of the landing pad. This piece does not require a beveled edge. It enables the house to be firmly screwed to the wall once it has been hung from the French cleat. For added support, use TimberLOK screws to securely attach the front, sides, and back of the bat house to the French cleat. Pre-drill holes to carefully avoid penetrating roosting chambers.

Buildings

Commercial suppliers of bat houses normally include mounting fasteners and instructions, especially for mounting on buildings. In fact, small houses should only be used on buildings to stabilize temperature. L-brackets are commonly provided. However, you have the option of extending your bat house from the building to which you are mounting. This provides an extra roosting space, including a cooler area of greater ventilation on hot days. To do this, simply cut two 3/4" to 7/8" x 2"

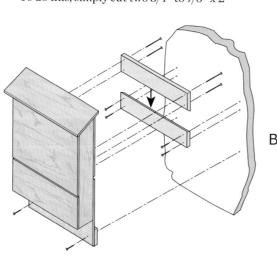

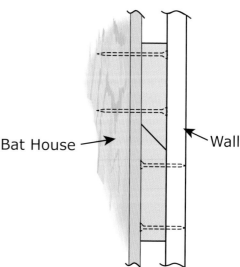

Bat House →   ← Wall

A wide variety of bats, such as this long-eared bat in Bulgaria, roost in woodpecker holes.

WHO CAN I ATTRACT?

Worldwide more than 70 species of bats have been attracted to artificial roosts, including more than a dozen in North America.

Throughout most of America, there are at least three species of bats that can be attracted to bat houses, often four or five in southern areas.

Brazilian free-tailed bats (*Tadarida brasiliensis*) range throughout most of the southern and western U.S., as well as Latin America. They traditionally formed colonies of millions in caves, but readily occupy man-made structures including bat houses. Their colonies in bat houses seem limited only by the size of the roost. Hundreds of thousands can be attracted to a single location. Some populations migrate south for winter, while those living in mild coastal climates, such as Florida, remain year-round.

Florida bonneted bats (*Eumops floridanus*) are known only from southern Florida where they are year-round residents. Traditional roosts were in woodpecker holes and beneath loose bark on snags. As these were lost, the species became endangered. They are now recovering through use of small bat houses. These are the largest U.S. bats known to use bat houses and prefer crevice widths of approximately 1-1/2".

Velvety free-tailed bats (*Molossus molossus*) are restricted to tropical and subtropical areas of North and South America. In the U.S., they are found only in the Florida Keys. Their original roosts were likely in snags and tree hollows, but they have readily adapted to living in buildings and are easily attracted to bat houses.

Pallid bats (*Antrozous pallidus*) live in arid and semi-arid areas of western North America, from south central British Columbia to Mexico. They form small colonies in rock crevices, buildings, bridges, and occasionally in bat houses. They are presumed to hibernate in rock crevices. They've declined in many areas, often from loss of roosts.

Big brown bats (*Eptesicus fuscus*) are found throughout most of North America, south to Columbia and Venezuela. They occur in most habitats, roost in a wide variety of tree cavities and rock crevices, form nursery colonies of up to 200 individuals, and are the most frequent bat house users. Their unique roost tolerance minimizes needs for seasonal migration to caves or abandoned mines, likely explaining their exceptional success in surviving where others cannot.

Evening bats (*Nycticeius humeralis*) range from Wisconsin and Pennsylvania, south through the Gulf States, and into northeastern Mexico. They traditionally roosted in tree cavities, but as these have been lost, they have gradually sought refuge in buildings. They are now also common occupants of bat houses, especially in the Gulf States. Colonies can include up to several hundred. Some are active year-round; those farther north migrate south for winter.

Little brown myotis (*Myotis lucifugus*) were once among the most abundant bats of the northern U.S. and Canada. Thousands could be attracted to a single location. However, white-nose syndrome (WNS) has caused an approximately 90% decline. Traditional summer roosts were in tree cavities near rivers or lakes. Bat houses are substantially aiding this species' recovery and have proven useful in monitoring status trends.

Northern long-eared myotis (*Myotis septentrionalis*) predominantly occur in northeastern North America but also range into the Southeast. Prior to WNS losses, these bats commonly shared bat houses with little brown myotis, though normally in much smaller numbers. This species is now federally listed as threatened in the U.S. Up to 100 or more have been reported in a single rocket box. Traditional summer roosts were in tree cavities. They leave in winter, but their hibernation needs are poorly understood.

Indiana myotis (*Myotis sodalis*) occur throughout eastern North America, occasionally as far south as Alabama and Georgia. They once ranked among America's most abundant bats, but through loss of key roosts in caves and snags they have declined dramatically. They are now federally listed as endangered. They traditionally formed huge aggregations in hibernation caves and often reared young beneath loose bark on snags, both of which are now in short supply. Rocket boxes can help in summer, but improved restoration and protection of hibernation caves is needed for full recovery.

Southeastern myotis (*Myotis austroriparius*) are found throughout much of the southeastern U.S., especially in the Gulf States. They traditionally formed colonies of many thousands in caves, but also reared young in tree hollows. As trees have been cleared and caves have been disturbed or destroyed, they have increasingly sought refuge in buildings near rivers where they feed. They are now also frequent bat house users.

Yuma myotis (*Myotis yumanensis*) range across western North America, from southern British Columbia to Arizona. They traditionally roosted in caves, tree hollows, and rock crevices, often in arid areas, but always near rivers or lakes. Many live in buildings or other man-made structures, and thousands have been attracted to bat houses at single locations.

Long-eared myotis (*Myotis evotis*) are found in western North America, from southwestern Canada to Baja California. They normally live in small groups in rock crevices and beneath loose bark. They occasionally use buildings and have been reported using bat houses.

California myotis (*Myotis californicus*) are most abundant in lowland arid areas in western America. They occur from Alaska to southern Mexico, forming small colonies, most often in cliff face crevices, behind loose tree bark, and in buildings. They also readily use bat houses.

Cave myotis (*Myotis velifer*) form isolated populations in Oklahoma and Kansas, Central and western Texas, southern Arizona, and southeastern California, south to Mexico and Central America. They were once one of the most abundant species in their range, but they have lost many of their traditional roosts in caves and are now in need of help. They readily occupy bat houses.

Bats carry pollen farther
than any other pollinator.

THE VALUE OF EXPERIMENTING

The shade, not the color, of a bat house determines its internal temperature.

Experimentation can pay big dividends. Once even a few bats have been attracted, you're set for serious testing. However, don't be confused by desperate bats who may quickly fill even the worst of houses.

The late Tony Kock (pictured right) built roosts from Styrofoam that he hung in his barn. He sealed and painted Styrofoam sheets, held together in a simple wooden framework without sides, top, or bottom. On extra hot days he noticed signs of overheating, so he installed a thermostat-controlled fan, which the bats clearly enjoyed. He gradually expanded his nursery colony to include several thousand little brown myotis. Prior to attracting bats, he normally found 1 to 3 corn earworm caterpillars per ear of corn in his garden. He rarely found any thereafter.

Observe your bats' behavior. If they're exposing themselves even on average days, they may simply need more room due to overcrowding. Alternatively, if exposing themselves only on hot days, they may need cooler homes (lighter colored, better vented, or in less sunny locations). Through careful observation you may de-duce their needs and tempt them to move.

Try offering houses of varied design or materials. Discovery of new products that are easier to use, less expensive, longer lasting, or simply more attractive to bats can be of great value. The most valuable discoveries come from testing just one variable at a time. There is still much to learn, and additional species need help.

You can also help bats by sharing your discoveries. Please let Merlin Tuttle's Bat Conservation know if you have had extraordinary success or failure. Did your bats make a clear choice between differently treated houses? Did changing the location, color, or design of your house or houses make a difference? Answers to such questions are important to helping bats.

NOVEL AMERICAN OPTIONS

Plastic Bat Houses

In Texas, the late Marvin Maberry, a retired public safety officer, developed successful, light-weight houses from plastic conduit that he flattened, welded, and coated with stucco to provide secure footing. His houses included several 3/4" round holes on each side, shielded from light and wasp entry. In some houses, he attempted to use sturdy, plastic mesh to form roosting partitions. These houses were successfully occupied by nearly twice the normal number of bats for a house of that size. However, the material eventually deteriorated, causing abandonment and in some cases injury to bats. Experimentation with stronger and better anchored materials has potential but requires thorough and long-term testing prior to being advocated for general use. Maberry also developed a type of "rocket box" constructed of a conduit tube slipped over a central pole and capped at the top.

California Plank Roosts

Cliff Fong, a California farmer, simply added several 3/4" furring strips beneath the sides and top of two 12" x 6' rough-sawn cedar planks. He attracted hundreds of Brazilian free-tailed bats and Yuma myotis to his tractor shed.

Cinderblock Tower Roosts

"Tower roosts" mimic the large tree hollows once used by the now uncommon Rafinesque's big-eared bat *(Corynorhinus rafinesquii)*, a state-listed threatened species. This lowland hardwood forest dweller once occupied tree cavities 3' to 6' wide by 9' to 12' tall in ancient gum and cypress trees. Tower roosts are built from cinder blocks arranged in a 4' square by 12' tall structure. They have been used from the Gulf States to Kentucky but failed to attract nursery colonies until pairs were provided, one cooler than the other, with black versus light-colored tops. Subsequently, colonies remained through entire summer seasons, some year-round, moving back and forth to meet seasonal needs.

Aluminum Shell Bat Boxes

The Pennsylvania Game Commission provides outstanding instructions for building bat boxes with an aluminum exterior. They are 28" tall by 7-1/2" wide, constructed from 1/8" aluminum welded into a long-lasting outer shell with 1/2" vent holes at 1" intervals across the sides and front, 10" from the bottom. For use in high elevations and cooler climates, the upper 14" and top are painted black. These houses accommodate six 1/4"-thick traditional-type, plywood roost partitions and have been highly successful in attracting big brown bats and little brown myotis. They also have accommodated Indiana myotis. For locations where these houses become overcrowded, instructions for double-wide houses are available (Photo courtesy of Bat Conservation and Management).

Artificial Bark

In Arizona, forestry biologists Garcia de la Cadena and Melissa Siders convinced a taxidermist friend to create artificial bark for bats. It was wrapped around tree trunks about 20 feet up, attached with deck screws and silicone. They successfully attracted nursery colonies of western bat species and the idea was quickly communicated to biologists in the East. It was tested as a means of helping threatened northern long-eared and endangered Indiana myotis. Initial success was achieved, but growth of living trees rendered attachments relatively short-lived. Eventually, artificial bark was wrapped around untreated utility poles embedded in concrete, but without chemical treatment the embedded ends of the poles too often deteriorated within 10 years. Experienced users found "Bat Bark" benefits were disappointingly brief and costly. Much remains to be accomplished for this approach to become practical for long-term use.

Artificial Cave

Millions of bats have lost former homes in caves. David Bamberger built an artificial cave on his ranch in Central Texas, which attracted a nursery colony of approximately 500,000 Brazilian free-tailed bats (pictured right). This structure is composed of 20 tons of rebar and 300 cubic yards of 12"-thick gunite. It is built in a ravine, equipped with drainage, and covered with earth. It covers 3,000 square feet and provides 8,000 square feet of roosting surface. Such projects require expert consultation on bat needs.

BAT HOUSES AROUND THE WORLD

Taiwanese Bat Houses

In Taiwan, a house weighing just 5 pounds was developed by a grade school teacher, Heng-Chia Chang. More than 4,000 of these houses have been sold for use on buildings, with proceeds supporting conservation. Landing and all roosting areas are cut, both horizontally and vertically, 1/8" deep at 3/4" intervals, providing extra secure footing. More than 100 were initially mounted at Chang's school, where students and teachers documented nearly 100% occupancy and nursery use by lesser Asiatic house bats (*Scotophilus kuhlii*) and Japanese pipistrelles (*Pipistrellus abramus*). In other parts of Taiwan, this unique design has attracted 10 additional species, including similar sized relatives of North America's big brown bats, little brown myotis, and pipistrelle bats. We are now presenting this design for first-time testing in America.

United Kingdom's Kent Bat Boxes

Kent bat boxes are just 8" x 20", have roost crevices 5/8" to 7/8" wide, and are made from rough-cut lumber. They only shelter small numbers of bats, mostly males, but building them is a popular activity for children (Photo courtesy of Daniel Whitby).

Maps are provided only to show areas we discuss, not the limits of actual or potential use.

European Woodcrete Bat Boxes

Woodcrete is a mixture of sawdust and concrete widely used for both bird and bat houses in Europe, often in managed forests where natural roosts are now scarce. These houses are made from casts, formed in two separate pieces. A removeable or hinged front permits cleaning. To produce woodcrete, soak fine sawdust overnight in a solution with detergent (not too frothy). Squeeze the moisture out, allow it to dry, then mix with cement (1 portion of cement to 3-1/2 of sawdust). This material is rough surfaced, reported to last 20 to 25 years, and provides extra insulation. Some houses are open inside for cavity roosting species. Many provide crevices with open bottoms. They are heavier than wooden houses and differ greatly in roost microclimate. Barbastelle bats (*Barbastella barbastellus*), when given a choice between woodcrete and wooden houses of the same design, chose only the latter, though brown long-eared (*Pleocotus auritus*), Bechstein's (*Myotis bechsteinii*), Natterer's (*Myotis nattereri*), and noctule bats (*Nyctalus noctule*) also accept woodcrete houses. These houses seldom accommodate more than 30 bats. It is unusual for European species to form colonies of over 100, even in buildings (Photo courtesy of Daniel Hargreaves).

Mediterranean Funnel Houses

When strategically distributed around Mediterranean rice paddies, funnel houses attracted sufficient soprano pipistrelle bats (*Pipistrellus pygmaeus*) to end the need for pesticides. Farmers noted that the cost of putting up bat houses was 6 to 8 times less than that of relying on chemical treatments. Such natural pest control is only feasible where there is native vegetation nearby for feeding between seasonal crop pest availability (Photo courtesy of Oriol Massana Valeriano).

Mekong Delta Palm Frond Roosts

Cambodian and Vietnamese farmers in the Mekong River Delta area have a long history of attracting bats to artificial roosts for the purpose of collecting guano, which is sold as fertilizer. They cut and dry the fronds of sugar palms and wire them in bundles of 4 to 5 fronds each, 10 bundles per tree, to form a dense skirt beneath the crown of the tree. One farmer reported earning nearly 900 U.S. dollars per year per roost, and that farmer had 10 roosts. Roosts attract thousands of lesser Asiatic yellow bats (*Scotophilus kuhlii*). Each roost must be replaced once or twice annually, as parasites build up and apparently force abandonment (pictured above). Farmers always have new roosts in place. They are undoubtedly benefiting from crop pest control, though most are as-yet unaware of this added reward.

Latin American Bat Towers

In Latin America, a German bat biologist, Detlev Kelm, created roosts from slabs composed of sawdust and concrete to successfully attract Neotropical fruit and nectar-eating bats to promote reforestation in clearings. These roosts also attracted a wider range of bats, including 10 species (Photo courtesy of Detlev Kelm).

Roosts are reached
by bamboo
ladders.

FREQUENTLY ASKED QUESTIONS

Millions of bats in warm climates now roost in bridges, mostly in crevices 3/4" to 1-1/2" wide and at least 12" deep. Where box-beam construction is used, ideal crevices are easily created at no extra cost.

What is the likelihood of attracting bats to my bat house? If bats are attempting to live in neighborhood buildings, success is highly probable. As with birds, there are no guarantees. However, occupancy rates often exceed 80% where well-made and sited houses are provided. Nearness to varied habitat and water helps. Success is almost certain where well-made houses are provided several weeks prior to an eviction from a nearby building.

How long does it take to attract bats to a bat house? In areas where bats have had prior experience, new bat houses often attract occupants within weeks. Where houses are newly introduced, 12 to 18 months is not uncommon. Much also depends on quality and placement. Approximately half of successful houses are used within 6 months, some within less than a month. If occupancy isn't achieved within 24 months, try moving the house into more or less sun. Some of America's most successful bat house users initially failed to attract bats but experimented until success was achieved.

How many bats can my bat house accommodate? That depends on the number, length, and width of roosting crevices in your house. Bats normally form a single, horizontal row in 3/4" wide roosting crevices. A horizontal foot of 3/4" wide roosting crevice can hold approximately 22 bats, varying slightly by species size. A 1 1/4" crevice can hold twice that number while forming a double row. Most North American species prefer 3/4" spaces, though colonies, even of small species, may expand into slightly wider crevices as they grow.

How effective are bats at controlling mosquitoes? No form of control is 100% effective. However, recent research has documented that several bat species feed heavily on mosquitoes, including kinds that carry West Nile virus. Bats can significantly reduce numbers of egg-laying females. Just one bat can catch 1,000 mosquito-sized insects in a single hour. Nevertheless, mosquito control should not be promised based solely on bats.

Can bats help protect my yard and garden from insect pests? Yes! Bats are important controllers of moths, plant hoppers, stink bugs, and other pests. They save American farmers billions of dollars annually in avoided insect damage and are ideal allies of organic farmers. Big brown bats from a single bat house can consume enough cucumber beetles in a summer season to prevent them from laying millions of eggs.

Can I entice bats to move out of my attic and into a bat house? They seldom, but sometimes, will relocate without exclusion, especially if a superior alternative is provided. Most relocations are successful if a quality bat house is provided a month or more in advance of an exclusion.

Will having bat houses in my yard interfere with attracting birds? No. Bats come out at night when birds are asleep. Just don't provide owl nesting boxes nearby if you are hoping to attract bats.

What are the odds of increased rabies risk? All mammals can contract rabies, but transmission from bats to humans is exceedingly rare, just one or two cases per year in the U.S. and Canada combined. Any human who simply doesn't attempt to handle bats is extremely unlikely to be bitten or to contract any disease from one. Americans are 20 times more likely to be killed by a neighborhood dog attack.

Why might bats NOT be attracted to my bat house? Too many cheaply marketed houses are uncaulked, sealed, or painted, are made of poor-quality materials, have roosting partitions too widely spaced, or have inadequate instructions. Additionally, some good houses are positioned to receive too little or even too much sun exposure, most often too little. Dramatic success has sometimes been achieved by simply moving a house a short distance into different sun exposure.

Millions of tourists have observed unforgettable emergences close-up in Austin, Texas, for decades without harm.

Why might bats have left my once-occupied bat house? In temperate regions, most bats will leave in fall and return in spring. However, they may depart early for a variety of reasons. These include inadequate temperature options, persistent owl or hawk predation, encroachment of vegetation, maintenance needs, or too many wasp nests. If problems are remedied, the bats normally return by the next season.

Can I harm bats by attracting them to a bat house that overheats on hot days or eventually deteriorates? Even natural roosts are often imperfect and ephemeral. Most bats that use bat houses originally lived beneath loose bark or in cavities in old snags, locations that often are short-lived. This likely helps explain bat preferences for locations where multiple roosts are available. As a colony expands, it eventually reaches roost carrying capacity. Overcrowding can kill young bats whether a roost is natural or artificial. If bats are rearing young in a roost that overheats on extra hot days, it is likely because they lack alternatives, not because they have been lured away from better roosts. They are best helped by providing more options.

Can special lures attract bats to my bat house? We are unaware of supporting evidence that bat lures effectively attract bats.

Will bats attract fleas or other parasites to my home? Like all animals, bats do have parasites, but they are highly host-specific and seldom bite humans except when a large nursery colony is excluded from a building, leaving starving parasites behind. No diseases have been reported to be transmitted by bat parasites.

How can I check my bat house for occupants? Try briefly reflecting sunlight from a mirror into a bat house to check for occupants. Alternatively, a bright flashlight can be used early or late in the day to avoid being dulled by sunlight. You may also place a light-colored cloth or plastic beneath and check for accumulating droppings. Eventually, you can count the emerging bats at dusk.

When is the best time to install a bat house? Bat houses can be installed at any time of year, but houses installed in fall or winter have several months to age and lose potentially offensive chemical odors before bats return in spring.

What do I do if I find a bat on the ground? Especially following periods of cold, rainy spring weather, mothers are sometimes forced to abandon pups due to lack of food. Alternatively, pups may be found beneath bat houses due to overcrowding during extreme heat. In either case, returning them to the bat house landing pad is likely futile, though it may make benefactors feel good. Wild animals, even bat pups, should not be handled without gloves. Call an animal rehabilitator for assistance.

Do bat droppings pose a health risk? Inhaling dust from any animal droppings can be hazardous and should be avoided. Bat droppings pose no greater risk than those from birds or cats.

Should I purchase a pup catcher? There is little evidence that pup catchers work as advertised. Pups may fall from roosts due to the death of mothers, overcrowding, or abandonment by mothers who can't find sufficient food during weather extremes. In such instances, returning pups to the roost is unlikely to help. Pups that have simply lost their footing may be rescued by their mothers if they can be left in a nearby location above ground level.

What other ways can I help bats? Share your knowledge with friends and neighbors. Help all wildlife by fostering native vegetation wherever possible. Ask conservation organizations you support, and your state department of wildlife, what they are doing to end the killing of millions of bats annually by careless use of wind turbines. Are they protecting key bat caves and other habitats essential to helping bats recover from WNS? Are they countering misleading disease warnings? *Stay well informed and only support those who are taking meaningful actions!*

Bat houses mounted on masonry
chimneys or walls provide extra
thermal stability preferred by bats
(Photo courtesy of Bat BnB).

CONSTRUCTION MATERIALS

All materials, including primers, paints, stains, and screws, must be exterior grade for outdoor use. If plastic is used for outer shells, it should be UV-resistant. Where natural wood color is appropriate, clear polyurethane can be substituted for a sealant or paint.

Lumber

A wide variety of lumber has been used successfully in bat houses. However, due to its convenient availability in large sheets, AC, BC, or T1-11 plywood, 1/2" to 5/8" thick, is most often used for fronts and backs. Roosting partitions are typically cut from 3/8" to 1/2" plywood, though heavier board lumber may better meet bat needs. Many exteriors are composed of several cedar boards, 1/2" to 3/4" thick by 6" to 12" wide. Cedar is often preferred by vendors for aesthetics, though many woods have been effectively used by private builders. Cuts that are smooth on only one side, turned rough-side-in, provide improved footing for roosting or landing bats. Lumber that is rough-cut on both sides is ideal for bats but is harder to work with and heavier. Used pallet wood may be available for free.

In Vermont, Barry Genzlinger had excellent success building bat houses from beveled cedar siding, with Cabot Solid Color Acrylic Stain applied to all surfaces. In the few cases where Dan Dourson uses a sealant, he recommends AGRA LIFE Lumber-Seal, a clear wood sealant which contains no toxic chemicals.

This well-vented design mimics a pair of back-to-back houses with a pole through the middle. It has proven highly successful in Florida.

Brackets aid in attachment and metal roofs shield against midday sun and extend house lifespan.

lin, a carcinogen. It reportedly dissipates quickly. However, off-gassing may sometimes account for delayed occupancy. The possibility has not been conclusively tested, though bat house users are unanimous in the opinion that bats are more rapidly attracted to older houses or ones made of older wood.

Dan Dourson has voiced concerns about off-gassing from any applied chemicals. He typically uses uncaulked, unpainted, mostly rough-cut, air-dried, inch-thick lumber for his rocket boxes. Poles are black locust, Osage orange, or oak, long-lasting hardwoods. Dourson's houses are simply made from the most readily available, lighter-weight lumber, mostly tulip poplar, hemlock, short-leaf, or pitch pine purchased directly and less expensively from local sawmills. Bats appear to prefer the easier-to-grip surfaces and greater thermal stability of thicker lumber. They may also favor the lack of chemical off-gassing.

John Chenger produces four-chamber houses encased in a vented outer shell of UV-resistant poly material. Interior roosting baffles are made of 3/8" thick yellow pine plywood. He also uses 1/2" thick, black plastic roofs on all his traditional wooden houses, for greater durability and heat retention.

Houses constructed of plywood or lumber less than 3/4" thick appear to be much more successful and longer lasting if caulked, primed, and coated with at least two applications of latex paint, stain, or polyurethane.

In western Pennsylvania, Terry Lobdell recommends rough-sawn, inch-thick lumber, both for outer surfaces and interior roosting partitions. He often gathers scrap wood from construction sites, including used pallet wood, white pine, and aspen. To extend lifespans of these houses, he stains them, then covers roofs and the upper third of fronts with pre-painted aluminum coil stock. He covers all four sides of rocket boxes, particularly to protect against woodpeckers. Users who have tested metal roofs are unanimous in reporting greatly extended house longevity.

Successful bat house builders who use untreated and unpainted wood, rely on thicker, often rough-cut lumber. They point out that all plywood contains forma-

Hardware
Deck screws are recommended because they do not require predrilling or countersinking. They make their own hole as they are driven in, have inconspicuous cutters so the heads can be driven flush with the wood, and are approved for outdoor use. Roofing screws with rubber washers are best for roofs.

Caulk and Glue
Any good exterior caulk that is long-lasting and has good adhesion can be used. Latex acrylic caulk has the advantage of water cleanup. A silicone caulk, "Lexel" manufactured by Sashco (part #13010), has exceptional adhesion and lifespan, and dries

Metal roofs reduce overheating and greatly extend bat house lifespan.

clear. All external seams and screw heads should be carefully caulked to extend house lifespan.

The following glues have been recommended: Loctite PL Max Premium for attaching metal roofs to wood and Titebond III for securing wood to wood. Screws or brads ensure tight bonding.

Commercial bat house builder Debbie Pikul Zent, in Austin, Texas, caulks, primes, and paints her plywood houses externally and seals landing areas and interiors with dark grey stain. She has experienced full-capacity occupancy in as little as a few days. Only further testing can suggest whether such bats are especially attracted to her well-painted and caulked houses or are just desperate for shelter.

Roofing

Metal roofs, whether galvanized or aluminum, should be sealed and painted to protect against corrosion and/or provide appropriate heat absorption.

Options for Modification

Though we have provided detailed instructions for several kinds of proven bat houses (see Appendix 2), most can be expanded to attract larger numbers of occupants. You may double the width of houses and mount them back-to-back in pairs with an extra roosting space in between to accommodate more bats with an improved temperature range. Taller houses increase temperature diversity while wider houses shelter more bats.

A cave myotis
about to devour
a June beetle.

BUILDER'S PLANS

SINGLE-CHAMBER STARTER HOUSE

Single-chamber houses, when properly mounted on buildings, are achieving encouraging success and provide easy, inexpensive opportunities for testing color and sun exposure in new locations. In moderate climates, they may also work well on poles when two houses are paired back-to-back. The materials we suggest provide an ideal compromise between cost, ease of construction, and bat needs. This house can shelter up to 40 bats.

Materials (for TWO single-chamber houses)
All materials must be outdoor rated. House dimensions and screw size may need to be adjusted based on available lumber thickness to provide an ideal roosting width of 3/4" to 7/8". Painting or use of a sealant is highly recommended for plywood houses and for any lumber less than 3/4" thick but may not be necessary for houses made of heavier lumber.

- 1 half sheet 5/8" thick T1-11, AC, or BC plywood
- 1 pine or cedar board, 1" x 4" x 6' (actual 3/4" x 3-1/2" x 6')
- 1 furring strip, 1" x 2" x 8' (actual 3/4" x 1-1/2" x 8')
- Deck screws: 1-1/2" and 1-1/4"
- 1 tube Titebond III glue
- 1 tube Lexel sealant

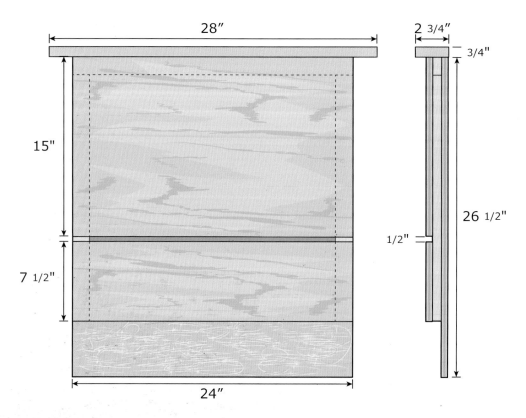

- Dark brown or black water-based stain for interior
- Wood stain, polyurethane sealant, or a combination of water-based primer and latex paint for exterior (color appropriate to climate and/or sun exposure)
- Optional: 2 Sealed and pre-painted aluminum coil foil pieces, each 5-1/2" x 28"

Cut list

- Roof (A): 3/4" x 4" x 28" cut from pine or cedar
- Back (B): 5/8" x 24" x 26-1/2"
- Top spacer (C): 3/4" x 1-1/2" x 24"
- Side spacers (D): 2 pieces, each 3/4" x 1-1/2" x 21-1/2"
- Top (front) (E): 5/8" x 15" x 24"
- Top (bottom) (F): 5/8" x 7-1/2" x 24"
- Square spacers (G): 2 pieces, each 3/4" x 1-1/2" x 1-1/2"

Instructions

1. Cut all pieces to size. Note: 1/2" vent may be unnecessary in cool climates.
2. If using AC or BC plywood, roughen all interior surfaces by hand scouring or cross-cutting grooves 1/32" deep at 3/4" intervals. Remove any rough edges or splinters and coat interior surfaces with 50% diluted wood stain to prevent light from reflecting into house.
3. On roughened surface of back piece (B), apply a bead of glue along top and sides where spacers (C & D) will be placed, not extending into landing area.
4. Place spacers over bead of glue.
5. On roughened surface of back piece (B), center square spacers (G) from side to side. Attach one 7-1/2" from the top, the other 7-3/4" from the bottom using 1-1/4" screws and glue.
6. Apply another bead of glue to spacers and attach front pieces (E & F) with roughened sides facing inward, leaving a 1/2" vent between E and F.
7. Align all external edges and screw into place using 1-1/2" screws. Turn assembly over and repeat from back side, staggering screws so they do not collide. We recommend pre-drilling to make screwing easier and to avoid splitting. Note: It is important to make sure screws do not protrude into roosting chambers. All screwheads and external seams should be sealed throughout construction.
8. Attach wooden roof (A) using 1-1/2" screws and glue.
9. Optional: To extend house lifespan, cover wooden roof with aluminum. Along both front and back edges of house, bend 3/4" 90° to fit tight with the roof. Attach aluminum using 1/2" screws.
10. Apply appropriately colored wood treatment to exterior—two coats of wood stain or polyurethane sealant, or a combined two coats of primer and three of paint.
11. Optional: Two houses can be attached by laying one atop the other with 3/4" spacers in between to create a three-chamber house. Cover with a roof to ensure it is leak and draft free.

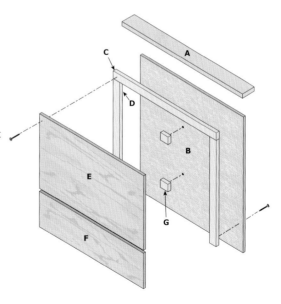

TRADITIONAL NURSERY HOUSE

The dimensions of this house have been chosen to conserve wood and facilitate construction. It can shelter nearly 100 bats. Expansion of either height or width is encouraged. In fact, this house has often been built with double or triple-wide dimensions, with two mounted back-to-back beneath a metal roof. Such expanded houses have attracted up to 1,000 free-tailed bats.

Materials

All materials must be outdoor rated. House dimensions and screw size may need to be adjusted based on available lumber thickness to provide an ideal roosting width of 3/4" to 7/8". Painting is highly recommended for plywood houses and for any lumber less than 3/4" thick but may not be necessary for houses made of heavier lumber.

- 1 half sheet 1/2" thick T1-11, AC, or BC plywood
- 1 pine or cedar board, 2" x 6" x 8' (actual 1-1/2" x 5-1/2" x 8')
- Sealed and pre-painted aluminum coil foil, 20-1/2" x 6-1/2"
- Deck screws: 1-1/4", 1-5/8", and 6"
- Roofing screws with rubber washers, 3/4"
- 1 tube Titebond III glue
- 1 tube Lexel sealant
- Dark brown or black water-based stain for interior

- Wood stain, polyurethane sealant, or a combination of water-based primer and latex paint for exterior (color appropriate to climate and/or sun exposure)

Instructions

1. Cut all pieces to size. Cut 3 vertical grooves into side pieces (D), 3/4" deep and 1/2" wide at 3/4" intervals. Note: 1/2" vent may be unnecessary in cool climates.

2. Roughen all interior surfaces by hand scouring or cross-cutting grooves 1/32" deep at 3/4" intervals. Remove any rough edges or splinters and coat interior surfaces with 50% diluted wood stain to prevent light from reflecting into the house.

3. Apply a bead of glue along full length of each side piece (D) before attaching back pieces (B & C) using 1/5-8" screws. Leave a 3/4" vent between B and C. Make sure

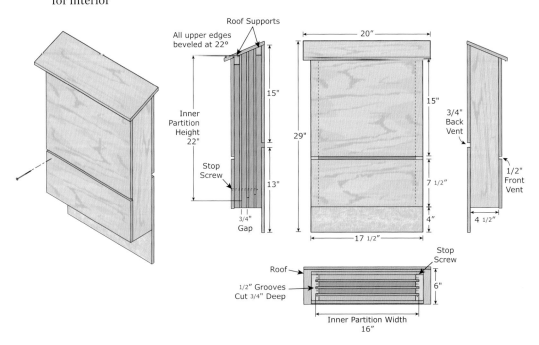

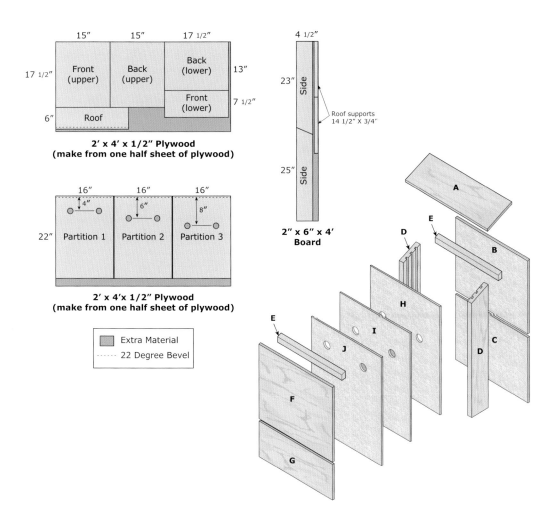

2' x 4' x 1/2" Plywood
(make from one half sheet of plywood)

15" — Front (upper) | 15" — Back (upper) | 17 1/2" — Back (lower)
17 1/2"
13"
7 1/2"
6" — Roof

2' x 4'x 1/2" Plywood
(make from one half sheet of plywood)

16" — Partition 1 (4") | 16" — Partition 2 (6") | 16" — Partition 3 (8")
22"

Extra Material
22 Degree Bevel

4 1/2"
23" — Side
25" — Side
Roof supports 14 1/2" X 3/4"

2" x 6" x 4'
Board

top angles match for a tight-fitting roof, sand if necessary. Note: It is important to make sure screws do not protrude into roosting chambers. All screwheads and external seams should be sealed throughout construction.

4. Attach first roof support (E) to upper edge of back piece (B), between side pieces (D) using glue and 1-1/4" screws.

5. Repeat steps 3 and 4 for attaching front pieces (F & G), leaving a 1/2" vent between, and second roof support (E).

6. Center wooden roof (A) from side to side and attach with 1-1/4" screws and glue. We recommend pre-drilling holes to avoid penetrating roosting chambers.

7. Lay assembly down and slide roosting baffles (H, I, & J) into side grooves. Fit baffles flush with roof. Secure baffles using one 6" screw on each side, making sure to penetrate each baffle. We recommend pre-drilling. This simple attachment style allows for easy baffle replacement and maintenance.

8. Apply sealant to all external seams, side joints, and screw heads.

9. Attach aluminum, centered over wooden roof, using 3/4" roofing screws with rubber washers.

10. Apply appropriately colored wood treatment to exterior—two coats of wood stain or polyurethane sealant, or a combined two coats of primer and three of paint.

ROCKET BOXES

Rocket boxes provide ideal temperature diversity, can be easily built, and mimic natural roosts. They allow bats to find preferred temperatures by moving vertically and/or by rotating horizontally into sun-exposed versus shaded sides. They tend to attract occupants faster but generally house fewer individuals. Rocket boxes are especially attractive to threatened northern long-eared and endangered Indiana myotis. Single-chamber rocket boxes generally house fewer than 20 bats, whereas double-chamber houses may shelter up to 100.

Single-chamber Rocket Box materials

All materials must be outdoor rated. House dimensions and screw size may need to be adjusted based on available lumber thickness to provide an ideal roosting width of 3/4" to 7/8". Full-dimension, rough-cut lumber from a local sawmill is preferred.

- 1 black locust or oak post (if available), 4" x 4" x 16' (actual 3-1/2" x 3-1/2" x 16')
Alternatively, 2 pine or cedar posts, 4" x 4" x 8' spliced together (see illustration)
- 2 pine or cedar boards, 1" x 8" x 8' (actual 3/4" x 7-1/4" x 8')
- Sealed and pre-painted aluminum coil foil, 7-1/4" x 7"
- Deck screws, 1-1/2"
- Roofing screws with rubber washers, 3/4"
- 1 tube Titebond III glue
- 1 tube Lexel sealant

- Wood stain, polyurethane sealant, or a combination of water-based primer and latex paint for exterior (color appropriate to climate and/or sun exposure)
- Optional: Dark brown or black water-based stain for interior

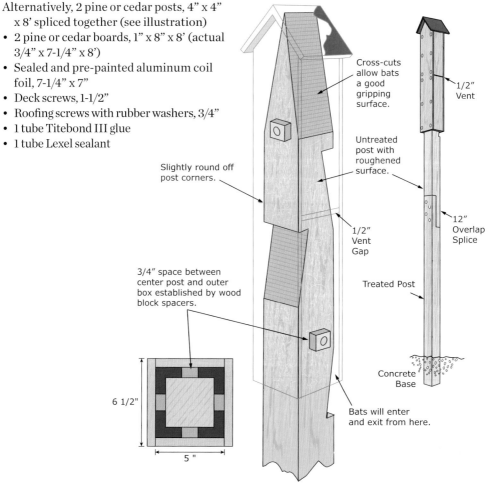

Cross-cuts allow bats a good gripping surface.

1/2" Vent

Untreated post with roughened surface.

Slightly round off post corners.

1/2" Vent Gap

12" Overlap Splice

3/4" space between center post and outer box established by wood block spacers.

Treated Post

6 1/2"

5 "

Concrete Base

Bats will enter and exit from here.

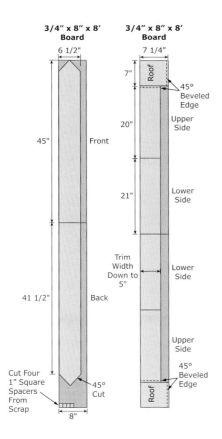

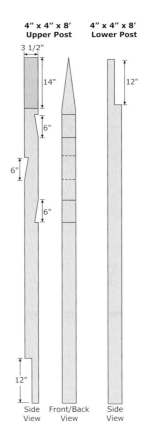

3/4″ x 8″ x 8′ Board — 6 1/2″, 45″, Front, 41 1/2″, Back, Cut Four 1″ Square Spacers From Scrap, 45° Cut, 8″

3/4″ x 8″ x 8′ Board — 7 1/4″, 7″, Roof, 45° Beveled Edge, Upper Side, 20″, Lower Side, 21″, Trim Width Down to 5″, Lower Side, Upper Side, 45° Beveled Edge, Roof

4″ x 4″ x 8′ Upper Post — 3 1/2″, 14″, 6″, 6″, 6″, 12″, Side View, Front/Back View

4″ x 4″ x 8′ Lower Post — 12″, Side View

Instructions

1. Cut all pieces to size. Note: 1/2″ vent may be unnecessary in cool climates. If a hardwood post is unavailable, splice together one 8′ pressure-treated and one 8′ untreated post, pressure treated post on bottom.

2. Cut top of post at a sharp angle and cut three notches, 6″ long by 1″ deep. Bottom notch is reversed for ease of entry and extends about 3″ below bottom of assembly. Slightly round off post corners.

3. Roughen uppermost 49″ of post and any smooth-cut interior surfaces. Within notches, cross-cut grooves 1/16″ deep at 3/4″ intervals. Hand scour remainder of post. Remove any rough edges or splinters. Optional: Coat first 6″ of interior surfaces with 50% diluted wood stain to prevent light from reflecting into house.

4. Attach spacers to post in opposing pairs with 1-1/2″ screws and glue. Pre-drill holes to avoid splitting.

5. To assemble outer shell, attach front, back, and side pieces using 1-1/2″ screws and glue, rough sides facing inward. Note: It is important to make sure screws do not protrude into roosting chambers. All screwheads and external seams should be sealed throughout construction.

6. Attach wooden roof using 1-1/2″ screws and glue, making sure pieces fit together tightly. We recommend carefully pre-drilling holes to avoid penetrating roosting chambers.

7. Apply sealant to all external seams, side joints, and screw heads.

8. Attach aluminum roof, centered over wooden roof, using 3/4″ roofing screws with rubber washers.

9. Apply appropriately colored wood treatment to exterior—two coats of wood stain or polyurethane sealant, or a combined two coats of primer and three of paint.

10. Gently slip outer shell over post and spacers.

Double-chamber Rocket Box materials

All materials must be outdoor rated. House dimensions and screw size may need to be adjusted based on available lumber thickness to provide an ideal roosting width of 3/4" to 7/8". Painting is highly recommended for plywood houses and for any lumber less than 3/4" thick but may not be necessary for houses made of heavier lumber.

- 1 quarter sheet 3/4" thick T1-11, AC, or BC plywood
- 2 pine or cedar boards, 1" x 12" x 8' (actual 3/4" x 11-1/4" x 8')
- 2 pine or cedar boards, 1" x 8" x 8' (actual 3/4" x 7-1/4" x 8')
- 2 pine or cedar boards, 1" x 4" x 8' (actual 3/4" x 3-1/2" x 8')
- 1 steel pole, 2" x 20' (2-1/8" outside diameter)
- Sealed and pre-painted aluminum coil foil, 12-1/2" x 12-1/2"
- Deck screws: 1-1/4" and 1-1/2"
- Roofing screws with rubber washers, 1"
- 1 carriage bolt with washer and nut, 1/4" x 4-1/2"
- 1 tube Titebond III
- 1 tube Lexel sealant
- Ospho rust inhibitor
- Kilz all-purpose primer
- Exterior latex paint
- Wood stain, polyurethane sealant, or a combination of water-based primer and latex paint for exterior (color appropriate to climate)
- Optional: Dark brown or black water-based stain for interior

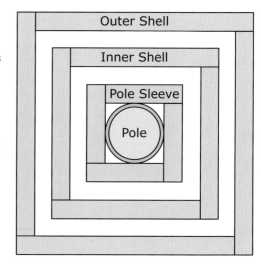

Instructions

1. Cut all pieces to size. Note: Vents may be unnecessary in cool climates.
2. Hand-roughen or cross-cut grooves 1/16" deep at 3/4" intervals on the smooth side of each 42" cedar or pine board. Remaining pieces should come rough on one side. Remove any rough edges or splinters. Optional: Coat first 6" of interior surfaces with 50% diluted wood stain to prevent light from reflecting into house.
3. To assemble pole sleeve, attach pieces using 1-1/2" screws and glue, rough sides facing outward. Attach spacers to pole sleeve using two 1-1/4" screws and glue per block. Pre-drill holes to avoid splitting. Note: It is important to make sure screws do not protrude into roosting chambers and all screwheads are sealed throughout construction. We recommend pre-drilling all holes.
4. To assemble inner shell, attach pieces using 1-1/2" screws and glue. Attach spacers to inner shell using two 1-1/4" screws and glue per block.
5. Slide inner shell over pole sleeve until top edges are flush. Attach the two using 1-1/2" screws. Secure from inner shell wall through uppermost pole sleeve spacer on each side of assembly. This will hold house together until roof is attached. Avoid collision with pre-existing screws.
6. To assemble outer shell, attach pieces using 1-1/2" screws and glue. Leave a 1/2" vent slot 12" from bottom on opposite sides. Rough sides should face inward.
7. Slide outer shell over inner shell until top edges are flush. Attach to inner shell using 1-1/2" screws. Secure from outer shell wall through uppermost

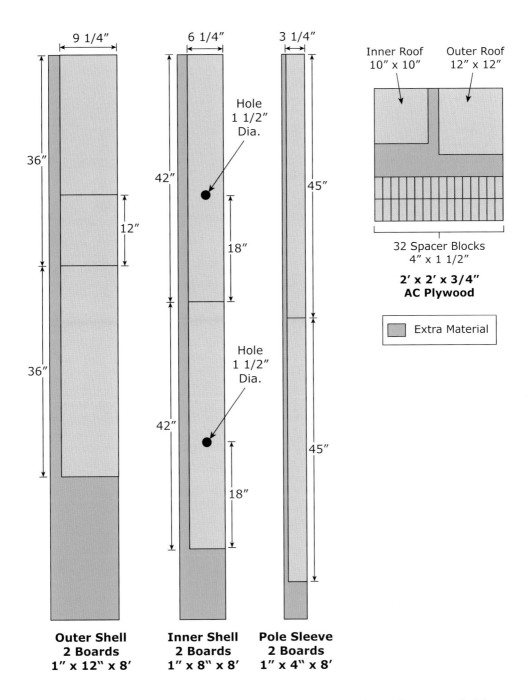

9 1/4"

6 1/4"

3 1/4"

Inner Roof
10" x 10"

Outer Roof
12" x 12"

Hole
1 1/2"
Dia.

36"

42"

45"

12"

18"

32 Spacer Blocks
4" x 1 1/2"

**2' x 2' x 3/4"
AC Plywood**

36"

Hole
1 1/2"
Dia.

Extra Material

42"

45"

18"

**Outer Shell
2 Boards
1" x 12" x 8'**

**Inner Shell
2 Boards
1" x 8" x 8'**

**Pole Sleeve
2 Boards
1" x 4" x 8'**

inner shell spacer on each side of assembly. Avoid collision with pre-existing screws.

8. Attach inner roof with 1-1/2" screws and glue, securing into outer shell walls.

9. Center and attach outer roof with 1-1/4" screws and glue, staggering screws to avoid colliding with those attaching inner roof.

10. Apply sealant to all external seams, side joints, and screw heads.
11. Center and attach aluminum over outer roof using 1" roofing screws with rubber washers.
12. Apply appropriately colored wood treatment to exterior—two coats of wood stain or polyurethane sealant, or a combined two coats of primer and three of paint.
13. Sand and coat metal pole with rust inhibitor. Then apply two coats of primer and two coats of latex paint. When dry, slide completed rocket box over pole.
14. Drill a 1/4" hole through both pole sleeve and pole, 1" from the bottom edge of completed assembly. Secure assembly to pole with one 4-1/2" carriage bolt, washer, and nut.
15. Repaint any scratched surfaces on pole after installation.

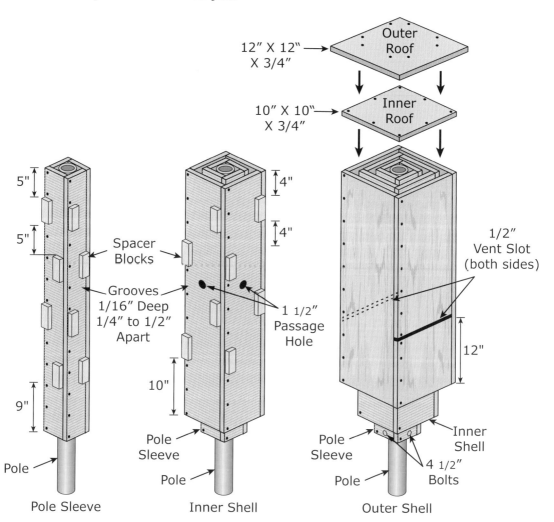

ZENT'S BAT CONDO

This house is essentially two single-chamber starter houses mounted 7/8" apart, front-to-front instead of back-to-back, except for repositioning of the vents. This provides a third especially well-ventilated roosting space and a sheltered landing area. When positioned to face southeast and northwest, covered by a metal roof, an exceptionally wide range of roosting temperature is provided. These houses are designed only for use on a pole and are ideally suited for moderate to hot climates. They can shelter up to 70 bats.

Materials

All materials must be outdoor rated. House dimensions and screw size may need to be adjusted based on available lumber thickness to provide an ideal roosting width of 3/4" to 7/8". Painting is highly recommended for plywood houses and for any lumber less than 3/4" thick but may not be necessary for houses made of heavier lumber.

- 1 half sheet 1/2" thick T1-11, AC, or BC plywood
- 2 pine or cedar boards, 1"x 6" x 8' (actual 3/4" x 5-1/2" x 8')
- 24-gauge galvanized metal roof, hemmed on front and back, 21" x 11" for cool climates, 21" x 13" for hot climates
- Deck screws: 1", 1-1/4", 1-5/8", and 2"
- Roofing screws with rubber washers, 3/4" to 1"
- Stainless steel brads, 1-1/4"
- 1 tube Titebond III glue
- 1 tube Lexel sealant
- Dark brown or black water-based stain for interior
- Wood stain, polyurethane sealant, or a combination of water-based primer and latex paint for exterior (color appropriate to climate and/or sun exposure)
- Ospho rust inhibitor, Kilz primer, and a light shade of exterior grade paint for treating metal roof

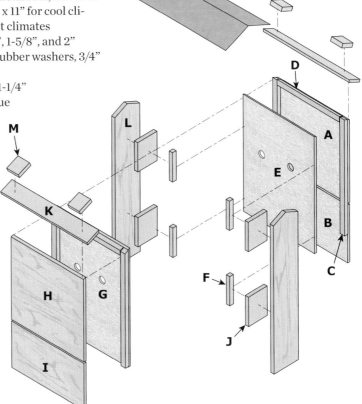

Cut list

(Pieces A, B, E, G, H, I, & K are cut from 1/2" plywood. Pieces C, D, F, J, L, M, & N are cut from 3/4" pine or cedar.)

- Back (top) (A): 16" x 15-7/8"
- Back (bottom) (B): 10" x 15-7/8"
- Full-length spacers (C): 4 pieces, each 20-1/2" x 1-1/4"
- Roof supports (D): 2 pieces, each 13-3/8" x 1-1/4"
- First interior baffle (E): 21-1/2" x 15-7/8"
- Short spacers (F): 4 pieces, each 5" x 1-14"
- Second interior baffle (G): 21-1/2" x 15-7/8"
- Front (top) (H): 16" x 15-7/8"
- Front (bottom) (I): 8" x 15-7/8"
- Vertical shade board supports (J): 4 pieces, each 4-3/8" x 5-1/2"
- Wooden roof (K): 2 pieces, each 20" x 3-1/4"
- Vertical shade board (L): 2 pieces, each 28" x 5-1/2"
- Roof spacers (M): 4 pieces, each 3" x 3"
- Back braces (N): 2 pieces, each 17-1/2" x 5-1/2"

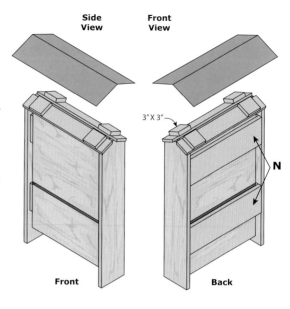

Instructions

1. Cut all pieces to size. Bevel all upper edges 25° for pieces A, C, D, E, G, H, K, & L. Note: Pass-through holes in pieces E & G should stagger to discourage wasp use.
2. Roughen all interior surfaces by hand scouring or cross-cutting grooves 1/32" deep at 3/4" intervals. Remove any rough edges or splinters from all pieces and coat interior surfaces with wood stain, diluted 50% for hand-scoured surfaces.
3. Place two full-length spacers (C) on a work bench. Lay back top (A) and bottom (B) over spacers, separated by 1/2". Align flush along edges and top and attach using 1" screws and glue or caulk. Note: It is important to make sure brads or screws do not protrude into roosting chambers and all screwheads are sealed throughout construction.
4. Carefully turn assembly over so that back pieces are now on bottom.

5. Attach one roof support (D) along top edge with 1" screws, fitting flush between spacers.
6. Place first interior baffle (E) over spacers. Align to create a sloping roof and attach using 1-5/8" screws and glue. Stagger screws to avoid collision with pre-existing screws.
7. Place two short spacers (F) over left and right edges of first baffle, fitting flush with top and bottom edges on each side.
8. Place second baffle (G) over short spacers, aligned at top with first baffle. Secure using 1-5/8" screws and glue, but only where supported by short spacers.
9. Place two full-length spacers (C) over left and right edges of second baffle. Attach second roof support (D) along top edge with 1" screws, fitting flush between spacers.
10. Place front top (H) and bottom (I) over spacers, separated by 1/2". Align to create a sloping roof and attach using 1-5/8" screws and glue or caulk. Stagger screws to avoid collision with pre-existing screws.

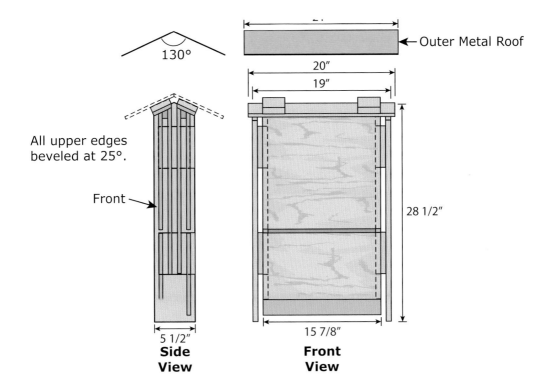

130°

All upper edges beveled at 25°.

Front

5 1/2"

Side View

← Outer Metal Roof

20"

19"

28 1/2"

15 7/8"

Front View

11. Install four vertical shade board supports (J), two on each side of assembly. Bottom of lower support should be flush with bottom of baffles, top of upper support should be 1-3/4" below top of front. Attach each support with two 1-5/8" screws and glue.

12. Align beveled edge of each wooden roof piece (K) 25° to fit flush vertically with edge of middle roosting chamber. This creates a 3/4" internal vertical access gap. Center over assembly and secure using 1-1/4" stainless steel brads and glue. Once glue sets, reinforce with 1-1/4" screws.

13. Turn assembly on one side and place a vertical shade board (L) over supports. Fit flush underneath wooden roof. Secure to shade supports using eight 2" screws and glue per side. Repeat on other side.

14. Place roof spacers (M) over wooden roof,

set in 2" from left and right edges. Attach each with two 1" screws and glue.

15. Install each back brace (N) using four 1-5/8" screws and glue, two screws per side. Secure from back into interior full-length spacers. Further secure with 2" screws through vertical shade boards into each end of back braces.

16. Apply sealant to all external seams, side joints, and screw heads.

17. Apply appropriately colored wood treatment to exterior—two coats of wood stain or polyurethane sealant, or a combined two coats of primer and three of paint.

18. Bend metal roof 130° in center to fit assembly. Prepare metal roof by applying Ospho, Kilz primer, and two coats of exterior paint.

19. Attach metal roof to roof spacers (M) using roofing screws with rubber washers.

LOBDELL'S THREE-CHAMBER HOUSE

This house has been highly successful in moderate climates but likely should be taller in hotter climates. The Lobdell bat house is typically made from random pieces of rough-sawn lumber that often can be salvaged from construction sites. It also can be built at nominal cost from cedar fencing, rough-cut on one side. Rough lumber provides excellent footing and increases thermal stability. Such houses are relatively heavy, but a French-cleat system can facilitate mounting.

The description below makes no assumptions about the size or number of lumber pieces that will be used. Simply arrange available lumber into the appropriate dimensions and include vent spaces where indicated. Some trimming may be required. Each layer of this bat house is added sequentially, like a multi-layered "sandwich," from back to front. This plan is for a three-chamber house but is easily adaptable to produce houses of one to four chambers.

Materials

All materials must be outdoor rated.
Note: This house may be modified to have a slanting roof. If so, all pieces that form the top of the house (A, C, E, G, I, J, and L) should be cut at a 45° forward-facing angle. These instructions assume the lumber used is 1" thick. If different, some measurements, including screw size, will need to be modified.

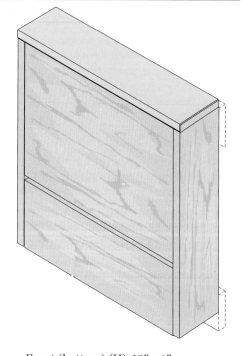

- Rough-cut 1" lumber or cedar fencing, cut and assembled to form the dimensions below (A-K)
- Rough-cut 3/4" lumber or cedar fencing for 6 spacers, dimensions below (L)
- Sealed and pre-painted aluminum coil foil, 20" x 7-3/4"
- Deck screws: 1-1/2", 1-5/8", and 2"
- Roofing screws with rubber washers, 2"
- 1 tube Titebond III glue
- 1 tube Lexel sealant
- Dark brown or black water-based stain for interior
- Wood stain, polyurethane sealant, or a combination of water-based primer and latex paint for exterior (color appropriate to climate and/or sun exposure)

Dimensions
- Back (top) (A): 18" x 15"
- Back (bottom) (B): 18" x 7"
- First interior baffle (top) (C): 18" x 14"
- First interior baffle (bottom) (D): 18" x 4"
- Second interior baffle (top) (E): 18" x 15"
- Second interior baffle (bottom) (F): 18" x 3"
- Front (top) (G): 18" x 16"
- Front (bottom) (H): 18" x 6"
- Ceiling (I): 2 pieces, 18" x 4-1/4"
- Sides (J): 2 pieces, approx. 22-1/2" x 6-1/4"
- Roof (K): 20" x 6-1/4"
- Spacers (L): 6 pieces, 20-1/2" x 1"

Instructions
1. Cut all pieces to size, except sides. Remove any rough edges or splinters and coat interior surfaces with 50% diluted wood stain to prevent light from reflecting into the house.

2. Attach ceiling pieces (I) to each other using 1-5/8" screws and glue, making sure they are aligned well to form a single, 2"-thick ceiling.
3. Attach ceiling to top of back (A) using 2" screws and glue, making sure all edges are exactly flush.
4. Lay out remaining lumber that will form top (A) and bottom (B) of back, allowing a 1/2" space for rear vent between A and B.
5. On left and right edges of assembly, lay spacers (L) that run from bottom of B flush to ceiling. Attach spacers with 1-1/2" screws and glue. Note: It is important to make sure screws do not protrude into roosting chambers. All screwheads and external seams should be sealed throughout construction.
6. Turn over assembly and secure with additional 1-1/2" screws from back into spacers. Then, turn assembly back over so that back is on bottom, and spacers are again on top.
7. Lay out lumber that will form top (C) and bottom (D) of first interior baffle over spacers, upper ends flush with ceiling. Leave a 3/4" space between C and D. These dimensions create an internal access space 1" lower than rear vent and are recessed 1-3/4" from bottom.
8. On left and right edges of assembly, lay spacers (L) that run from bottom of assembly flush to ceiling. Attach spacers with 1-1/2" screws and glue.
9. Next, lay out lumber that will form top (E) and bottom (F) of second interior baffle over spacers (L), upper end flush with ceiling. Leave a 3/4" space between E and F. These dimensions create an internal access space 2" lower than rear vent and are recessed 1-3/4" from bottom.
10. On left and right edges of assembly, lay spacers (L) that run from bottom of assembly flush to ceiling. Attach spacers with 1-1/2" screws and glue.
11. Finally, lay out lumber that will form top (G) and bottom (H) of front over spacers, upper end flush with top of assembly.

Leave a 1/2" vent space between G and H. Attach pieces with 2" screws and glue.
12. Cut sides (J) to fit assembly. Depending on final dimensions, sides will be about 6-1/4" x 22-1/2". Attach sides using 2" screws and glue. Screw into front, back, and ceiling.
13. Attach roof (K) to ceiling (I) using 1-5/8" screws and glue.
14. Apply sealant to all external seams, side joints, and screw heads.
15. Center aluminum over wooden roof. Along both front and back edges of assembly, bend 3/4" 90° to fit tight with roof. Attach aluminum using 2" roofing screws with rubber washers.
16. Apply appropriately colored wood treatment to exterior—two coats of wood stain or polyurethane sealant, or a combined two coats of primer and three of paint.
17. Terry Lobdell uses a French cleat mounting system for poles and vertical spacer strips for buildings and chimneys. For added support when pole mounting, he recommends securing roof to pole using a heavy duty, metal L bracket.

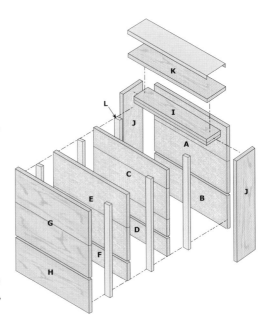

TAIWANESE HOUSE

In Taiwan, this uniquely small and light-weight bat house has been highly successful and exceptionally popular. It has attracted nursery groups of 6 to 12 bats, including 10 species. It is here recommended for first time testing in America, to be mounted only on buildings.

The original Taiwanese houses are cut from 1/2" thick Taiwania wood. Woodworking experience is required.

Materials
All materials must be outdoor rated. House dimensions and screw size may need to be adjusted based on available lumber thickness to provide an ideal roosting width of 3/4" to 7/8".
- 1 pine or cedar board, 1" x 12" x 4' (actual 3/4" x 11-1/2" x 4')
- Stainless steel brads or staples, 1-1/2"
- Deck screws, 5/8"
- 1 tube Titebond III glue
- 1 2" stainless steel hinge, such as National Hardware N276-964 V514
- 1 small hasp lock, such as HL Electronic Business 2.2"
- Dark brown or black water-based stain
- Wood stain, polyurethane sealant, or a combination of water-based primer and latex paint for exterior surfaces (color appropriate to climate and/or sun exposure)

Cut list
- Roof (A): 10-1/2" x 1-1/2"
- Back (B): 9-1/2" x 15-1/2"
- Sides (C): 2 pieces, see diagram for dimensions
- Interior baffles (D): 3 pieces, see diagram for dimensions
- Door frame (E): 2 pieces, 1-1/4" x 7-1/2"
- Door (G): 9" x 4"
- Front (H): 9-1/2" x 10"

Instructions
1. Cut all pieces to size. For side pieces (C), there is a 90° angle between 10-1/2" edge and 2" edge. Following diagram clockwise, remaining angles are 136°, 103°

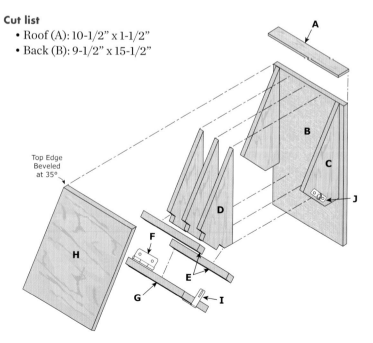

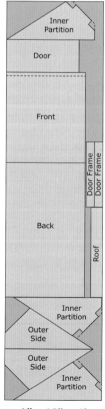

1" x 12" x 4'
Cedar or Pine Board

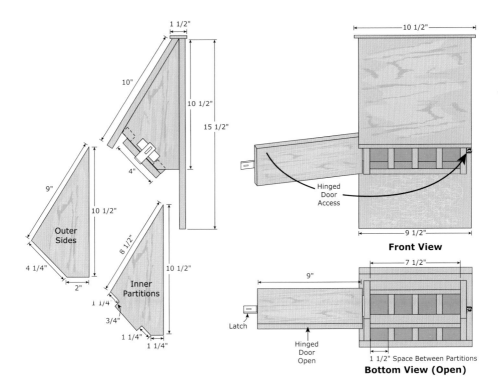

1 1/2"

10"

10 1/2"

15 1/2"

4"

9"

10 1/2"

Outer Sides

4 1/4"

2"

8 1/2"

10 1/2"

Inner Partitions

1 1/4

3/4"

1 1/4"

1 1/4"

Front View

10 1/2"

Hinged Door Access

9 1/2"

Bottom View (Open)

7 1/2"

9"

Latch

Hinged Door Open

1 1/2" Space Between Partitions

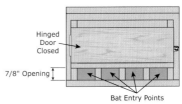

Bottom View (Closed)

Hinged Door Closed

7/8" Opening

Bat Entry Points

and 31°. Interior baffles are cut to same dimensions as sides but have notches that are 1/2" deep. Upper notch is 1" in length, lower notch is about 1/2"—just enough to give an entrance of 7/8".

2. Cross-cut grooves 1/8" deep at 3/4" intervals (both horizontally and vertically) for landing and roosting areas. Remove any rough edges or splinters and coat interior surfaces with 50% diluted wood stain to prevent light from reflecting into house.

3. Using stainless steel brads or staples and glue, attach sides (C) to back (B). Sides should be flush with top of back and a 1/2" in from edges. Note: It is important to make sure brads or staples do not protrude into roosting chambers.

4. Measure from inside of one side to inside of other (about 8") and position three interior partitions (D) to make four equal cavities, each about 1-1/2" wide. Attach partitions with brads or staples and glue, making sure they are flush with the top.

5. Attach two door framing pieces (E) with brads or staples and glue.

6. Attach door (G) with 5/8" screws using a hinge (F) and hasp latch (I and J).

7. Attach front (H) with brads or staples and glue, beveled to fit flush with roof.

8. Using brads or staples and glue, attach roof (A) to intersection of front and back at top of assembly

9. Apply sealant to all external seams and side joints.

10. Apply appropriately colored wood treatment to exterior—two coats of wood stain or polyurethane sealant, or a combined two coats of primer and three of paint.

ACKNOWLEDGMENTS

Brazilian free-tailed bats from Bracken Cave help Texas farmers by consuming tons of insect pests nightly.

This resource would have been impossible without decades of shared experience from 12 of America's most knowledgeable bat house innovators. Contributing experts include Frank Bibin of Georgia; Kent Borcherding of Wisconsin; Cal Butchkoski, John Chenger, and Terry Lobdell of Pennsylvania; Zack Couch and Dan Dourson of Kentucky; Thomas and Laura Finn of Florida; Barry Genzlinger of Vermont; and Rachel Long and Greg Tatarian of California. Daniel Hargreaves and Daniel Whitby provided additional understanding of bat house use in the U.K.

We thank Robin Eastham for a generous grant, matched by additional funds from Mindy Vescovo, Jeff Acopian, and Marshall and Jane Steves. We also thank Cal Butchkoski, John Chenger, Dan Dourson, Thomas and Laura Finn, Barry Genzlinger, and Terry Lobdell for peer review.

Walter Stewart, Mary Smith, and Terry Lewis provided invaluable testing and editorial review. David Chapman contributed bat house illustrations. Ed Corey, Jon Gillespie, Dave Johnston, Heather Kaarakka, Paul White, Joy O'Keefe, and Dan Saunders generously shared their insights. We also thank Austin Batworks, Bat BnB, Bat Conservation and Management, Bats Birds Yard, Habitat for Bats, and Fly by Night, inc. for their additional assistance.

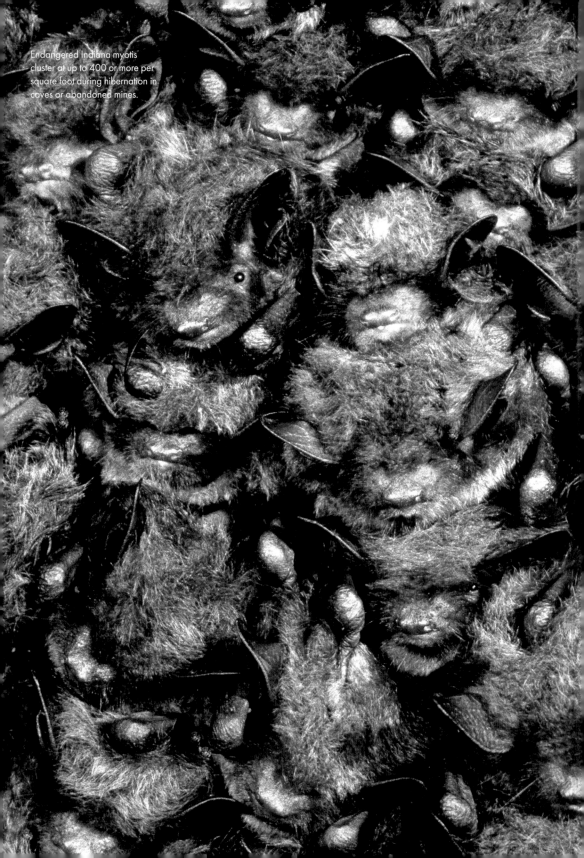

Endangered Indiana myotis cluster at up to 400 or more per square foot during hibernation in caves or abandoned mines.

A California
leaf-nosed bat
catching a cricket.